Iziane Castro Marques

THE STORY OF THE ATLANTA DREAM

Aari McDonald

WNBA: A HISTORY OF WOMEN'S HOOPS

THE STORY OF THE

ATLANTA
DREAM

JIM WHITING

Angel McCoughtry

CREATIVE EDUCATION / CREATIVE PAPERBACKS

Published by Creative Education and Creative Paperbacks
P.O. Box 227, Mankato, Minnesota 56002
Creative Education and Creative Paperbacks are imprints of
The Creative Company
www.thecreativecompany.us

Design and production by Blue Design (www.bluedes.com)
Art direction by Rita Marshall

Photographs by Getty (Brandon Bell, Tim Clayton/Corbis, Scott
Cunningham, Hannah Foslien, Icon Sportswire, Meg Oliphant, Abbie Parr)

Library of Congress Cataloging-in-Publication Data
Names: Whiting, Jim, 1943- author.
Title: The story of the Atlanta Dream / by Jim Whiting.
Description: Mankato, Minnesota : Creative Education and Creative
    Paperbacks, [2024] | Series: Creative Sports. WNBA : A History of
    Women's Hoops. | Includes index. | Audience: Ages 8-12 | Audience:
    Grades 4-6 | Summary: "Middle grade basketball fans are introduced to
    the extraordinary history of WNBA's Atlanta Dream with a photo-laden
    narrative of their greatest successes and losses"-- Provided by
    publisher.
Identifiers: LCCN 2022034156 (print) | LCCN 2022034157 (ebook) | ISBN
    9781640267169 (library binding) | ISBN 9781682772720 (paperback) | ISBN
    9781640008670 (adobe pdf)
Subjects: LCSH: Atlanta Dream (Basketball team)--History--Juvenile
    literature.
Classification: LCC GV885.52.A65 W55 2023 (print) | LCC GV885.52.A65
    (ebook) | DDC 796.323/6409758231--dc23/eng/20220720
LC record available at https://lccn.loc.gov/2022034156
LC ebook record available at https://lccn.loc.gov/2022034157

Printed in China

Angel McCoughtry

CONTENTS

LEGENDS OF THE HARDWOOD

Brittney Sykes

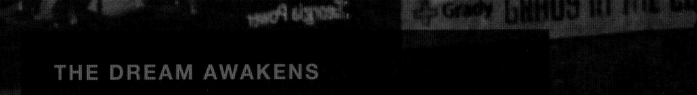

THE DREAM AWAKENS

The Atlanta Dream led the heavily favored New York Liberty by 14 points. It was late in the second quarter of the second game of the 2010 Women's National Basketball Association (WNBA) Eastern Conference finals. Atlanta had won the first game. With one more win, they would go to the WNBA Finals. The Liberty battled back. They tied the score 73–73 at the end of the third quarter. New York took a one-point lead three minutes into the fourth quarter. A few seconds later, forward Angel McCoughtry hit two free throws to put Atlanta back in front. The Dream slowly pulled away. McCoughtry had a three-point play with a minute remaining. It sealed Atlanta's 105–93 victory. Her 42 points are a WNBA playoff scoring record. The Dream would face the Seattle Storm for the league title!

Hardly anyone could have foreseen this level of success during the team's first season of play just two years earlier. Team officials chose the name Dream.

LEGENDS OF THE HARDWOOD

SANCHO LYTTLE
FORWARD
HEIGHT: 6-FOOT-5
DREAM SEASONS: 2009–17

A FAST LEARNER

Sancho Lyttle was born on a Caribbean island. She never played basketball until her family moved to the United States. Instead, she ran track and played net ball. That is a game in which teams pass the ball around and try to score goals. A Texas junior college coach taught her how to play basketball because of her obvious athleticism. It was a slow process. "My first year there, all I did was run the floor, post up, run the floor, defend, run the floor, post up," she said. "But the second year I started moving around more." She moved to the University of Houston. Lyttle became the school's all-time rebounds leader. Then she played four years with the WNBA's Houston Comets. When the team folded, she went to Atlanta. She was an All-Star in 2009. She was also a six-time member of the All-WNBA Defensive Team.

Sancho Lyttle

The team's name honored Civil Rights leader and Atlanta native Martin Luther King Jr. and his iconic 1963 "I Have a Dream" speech.

The Connecticut Sun drubbed the Dream 100–67 in the first game of their history. Atlanta lost to the Houston Comets nearly seven weeks later. It was the Dream's 17th defeat in a row. That set a league record for consecutive losses to start the season.

Chicago nearly kept the streak going. The Sky led by a point with less than two minutes left. Then Dream forward Tamera Young scored five points. Guard Ivory Latta added four more. Atlanta won 91–84. The losing streak was over. The Dream won just three more games the rest of the season. Their 4–30 record is one of the worst in WNBA history. "Basically, what we had was a bunch of young players that played hard but were just not good enough yet," said coach Marynell Meadors.

The dismal record gave Atlanta the first overall pick in the 2009 WNBA Draft. They took Angel McCoughtry. She had been a star at the University of Louisville. Meadors added several experienced players. They included small forward Chamique Holdsclaw, forward Sancho Lyttle, and guard Coco Miller. They opened the 2009 season with an 87–86 double-overtime win over Indiana. It gave notice to the league that they would be facing an improved Atlanta team. The Dream finished 18–16. They tied the Detroit Shock for second place in the Eastern Conference. The 14-win improvement from one season to the next helped make Meadors WNBA Coach of the Year. McCoughtry averaged nearly 13 points a game. She was named WNBA Rookie of the Year. Atlanta faced Detroit in the conference semifinals. The Shock swept the best-of-three series.

ALMOST TO THE SUMMIT

Atlanta built on a solid foundation in 2010. They opened the season with a six-game winning streak. Later on, they were 18–9. They were contending for first place in the conference. But the Dream lost six of their final seven games. They finished 19–15. Atlanta was fourth in the conference. McCoughtry was third in the league in scoring with an average of 21.1 points per game. Veteran forward/guard Iziane Castro Marques averaged nearly 17 points a game.

The Dream faced the Washington Mystics in the conference semifinals. Atlanta won Game 1. They scored 33 points in the second quarter outburst in Game 2. The Dream went on to crush the Mystics 101–77. They swept the best-of-three series. They narrowly beat the Liberty in Game 1 of the conference finals. Atlanta rode McCoughtry's 42 points in Game 2 to sweep that series too.

Atlanta advanced to the WNBA Finals for the first time. They faced Seattle. The Storm's 28 wins tied for the best record in WNBA history at that time. Seattle guard Sue Bird sank a jump shot with 2.6 seconds left in Game 1. It gave the Storm a 79–77 win. Seattle won the next two games with identical 87–84 scores. They swept

Iziane Castro Marques

the best-of-five series. "I think we have grown up quite a bit this season," said Meadors. "Maybe another minute on the clock might have made a difference in the outcome of this game and the same thing with the two games in Seattle."

The Dream lost 9 of their first 12 games in 2011. They went 17–5 the rest of the way. Their 20–14 record is second-best in team history. The Dream swept Connecticut in two close games in the conference semifinals. They lost Game 1 in the conference finals to the Indiana Fever. Atlanta won the next two. They advanced to the WNBA Finals for the second year in a row. They faced the powerful Minnesota Lynx, who had gone 27–7.

Minnesota had a 13–0 run at the start of the fourth quarter in Game 1. It broke open a tight game. They cruised to an 88–74 victory. The Lynx won Game 2, 101–95.

Angel McCoughtry

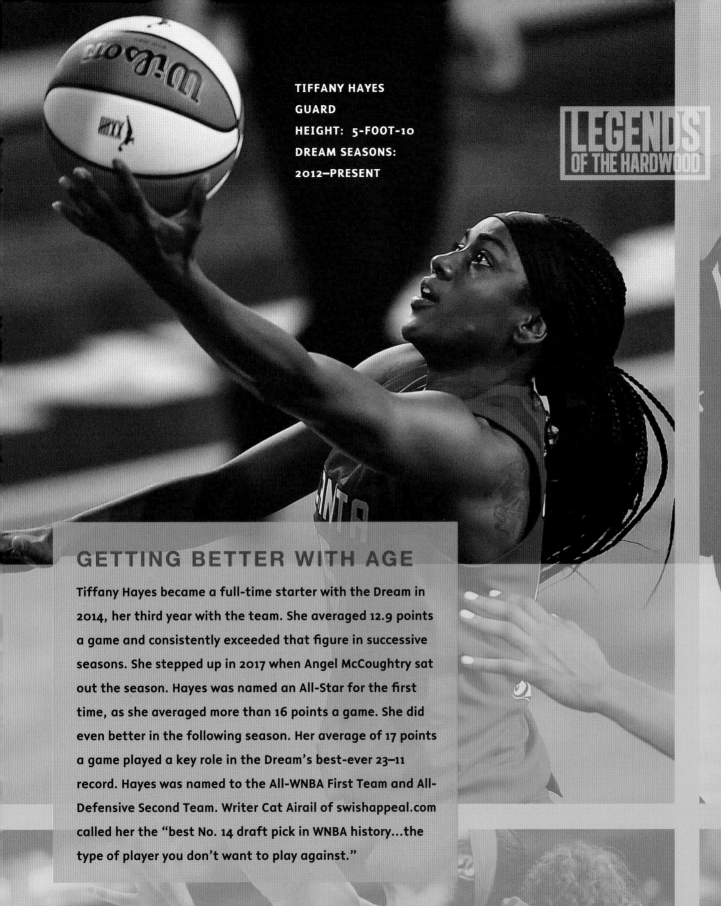

TIFFANY HAYES
GUARD
HEIGHT: 5-FOOT-10
DREAM SEASONS:
2012–PRESENT

GETTING BETTER WITH AGE

Tiffany Hayes became a full-time starter with the Dream in 2014, her third year with the team. She averaged 12.9 points a game and consistently exceeded that figure in successive seasons. She stepped up in 2017 when Angel McCoughtry sat out the season. Hayes was named an All-Star for the first time, as she averaged more than 16 points a game. She did even better in the following season. Her average of 17 points a game played a key role in the Dream's best-ever 23–11 record. Hayes was named to the All-WNBA First Team and All-Defensive Second Team. Writer Cat Airail of swishappeal.com called her the "best No. 14 draft pick in WNBA history...the type of player you don't want to play against."

ATLANTA DREAM

15

Érika de Souza

LEGENDS
OF THE HARDWOOD

ÉRIKA DE SOUZA
FORWARD/CENTER
HEIGHT: 6-FOOT-5
DREAM SEASONS:
2008–15

FROM POVERTY TO ALL-STAR

Érika de Souza grew up in poverty in Brazil. When she was 16, her mother encouraged her to play basketball. She played a single season with the Los Angeles Sparks in 2002 but had little playing time. She spent the next five years in Europe, improving her game. De Souza signed with the Connecticut Sun in 2007. Again she didn't play much. She came to Atlanta in the 2008 WNBA Expansion Draft. She became one of the cornerstones of the franchise. De Souza played a vital role in the Dream's three WNBA Finals appearances and was a three-time All-Star. She averaged 12.3 points, 8.5 rebounds, and 1.4 blocks per game.

Atlanta led by four points at halftime in Game 3. Minnesota's smothering defense held the Dream to just eight points in the third quarter. Atlanta came within one point of retaking the lead in the fourth quarter. The Lynx hung on for a 73–67 win. They swept the series.

Atlanta finished 19–15 in 2012. McCoughtry became just the second player to lead the league in both scoring and steals. Guard Tiffany Hayes was named to the WNBA All-Rookie First Team even though she didn't start for much of the season. Veteran point guard Lindsey Harding averaged more than 12 points per game. Atlanta defeated Indiana 75–66 in Game 1 in the conference semifinals. Indiana rode a 31-point third quarter to win Game 2. The Fever won Game 3. They won the series.

STARTING TO SLIDE

Atlanta jumped out to a 10–1 record to start the 2013 season. But they had four losing streaks of four games apiece later on to finish 17–17. That record was good enough for second place in the conference. Atlanta lost Game 1 of the conference semifinals against Washington. The Dream held the Mystics to just 45 points to easily win Game 2. The Dream's 80–72 win in Game 3 took the series.

Game 1 against the WNBA defending champion Fever in the conference championship series went back and forth. There were numerous lead changes.

A McCoughtry free throw gave Atlanta a 4-point lead with 16 seconds left. The Dream won 84–79. Tight Atlanta defense held the Fever to 53 points in Game 2. They won the conference championship.

For the third time in four years, Atlanta advanced to the WNBA Finals. Again they faced Minnesota. The Lynx mauled the Dream 84–59 in Game 1 and 88–63 in Game 2. Game 3 was more competitive. Atlanta trailed by just three points at halftime. That was as close as they could get. Minnesota won 86–77.

Atlanta played well for much of the 2014 season. At one point the Dream held a 15–5 record. But they faded to finish 19–15. The Dream still won the conference championship. Atlanta faced Chicago in the conference semifinals. The teams split the first two games. Atlanta held a 16-point lead after three quarters of the deciding Game 3. The Sky battled back to tie the score. Atlanta took an 80–77 lead with 29 seconds left. But the Sky scored twice. The second score came with just 8.4 seconds remaining. McCoughtry put up a shot as time expired. It bounced off the rim three times but didn't go in. Chicago won 81–80. It was the largest fourth-quarter playoff comeback in league history. "I think we got away from what we were doing well," Dream coach Michael Cooper said. "Our defense kind of got away from us."

Atlanta had just their second losing season in 2015. The low point came on August 7. A 29-point loss to the Fever was their sixth defeat in a row. It dropped them to 7–14. Atlanta played better the rest of the way. But they finished 15–19. They missed the playoffs for the first time in seven seasons.

Angel McCoughtry

ELIZABETH WILLIAMS
CENTER/FORWARD
HEIGHT: 6-FOOT-3
DREAM SEASONS: 2016–21

WHAT A DIFFERENCE A YEAR MAKES!

The Connecticut Sun made Elizabeth Williams the fourth overall pick in the 2015 WNBA Draft. She didn't live up to expectations. She averaged only about three points a game. "I was timid," Williams said. Then she was injured. Before the 2016 season, she was traded to the Dream. "That turned out to be exactly the restart I needed," she said. She became an instant starter. Williams averaged nearly 12 points and 8 rebounds a game that season. She was named as the WNBA Most Improved Player. She was an All-Star in 2017. Williams was named to the WNBA All-Defensive First Team in 2020.

TRYING TO COME BACK

The team added center/forward Elizabeth Williams for the 2016 season. Williams helped Atlanta burst out with six wins in the first seven games. But soon afterward, a six-game losing streak dropped the Dream to 8–9. They hovered around .500 for the rest of the season. They finished 17–17. The WNBA had adopted a new playoff format. The first and second rounds consisted of a single game. Atlanta defeated the Storm 94–85 in the first round. But they lost to the Sky in the second round, 108–98.

Atlanta had another strong start in 2017. They won four of their first five games. But McCoughtry was exhausted due to playing year-round with both the Dream and a Russian team for several years. She sat out the entire season. "Who can play basketball all year with no break for years and years and years?" she said. "We're not machines, we're not robots…you really need that time off just for your mental, number one, and then for your body."

Without her, Atlanta couldn't maintain their initial momentum. They had a nine-game losing streak during the season. They finished 12–22. The Dream was fifth in the Eastern Conference. It was the second-worst mark in team history. Atlanta missed the playoffs for the second time in three seasons. Rookie shooting guard/small forward Brittney Sykes averaged nearly 14 points a game. She was named to the WNBA All-Rookie First Team. Her season total of 471 points was a Dream rookie record.

McCoughtry returned for the start of the 2018 season. Even so, Atlanta got off to a slow start. By the end of June, they were just 7–8. They turned it around in July with an eight-game winning streak. There was another a streak of six wins in August. Even though McCoughtry suffered a serious knee injury near the end of the season, the Dream won the Eastern Conference title with a 23–11 mark.

That was—and still is—the best record in team history. It was only the second time that the Dream had won 20 games or more in a season. Nicki Collen was named WNBA Coach of the Year. It was her first head coaching job at any level. The Dream had a double bye in the playoffs. They faced the Mystics in the league semifinals in a best-of-five series. Washington won the first game, 87–84. The Dream won the next two games. The Mystics easily won Game 4. Atlanta took a one-point lead into halftime in Game 5. But a late Washington 9–0 run sealed an 86–81 victory for the Mystics.

LOOKING TO IMPROVE

McCoughtry missed the entire 2019 season due to lingering effects of her injury. Atlanta started with just 2 wins in the first 10 games. Things got even worse. The Dream had a 12-game losing streak from mid-July to late August. They finished the season with a WNBA-worst 8–26 record.

Due to the COVID-19 pandemic, the WNBA played the entire 2020 season in isolation in Bradenton, Florida. No spectators were allowed. The schedule was

Aari McDonald

ATLANTA AT NEW YORK
AUGUST 12, 2018

LEGENDS
OF THE HARDWOOD

THREE'S COMPANY

The Liberty took an 11-point lead into halftime. Just over a minute into the third quarter, Dream guard Renee Montgomery sank a 24-foot three-point jump shot. That ignited a streak of 18 more unanswered points. Montgomery contributed two more threes during that run as Atlanta took a 59–51 lead. Montgomery had two more three-pointers before the period ended. She opened the scoring in the fourth quarter with her sixth three-pointer. She added one more before the game ended with an 86–77 Dream win. Montgomery's seven three-pointers in a single half set a WNBA record. She had one in the first half. Her game total of eight tied a WNBA record. Less than three years later, she became a part-owner of the Dream.

ATLANTA DREAM

shortened to 22 games. The Dream finished 7–15, 10th overall. They were two games behind the Mystics for the eighth and final playoff spot. Rookie guard Chennedy Carter led the team in scoring with more than 17 points a game.

Atlanta began the 2021 season by winning four of their first six games. They faltered after that. The Dream finished with a seven-game losing streak. The final 8–24 mark was the third time in a row they missed the playoffs. Guard Aari McDonald provided one of the few bright spots. She had been the third overall pick in the 2021 WNBA Draft. She came off the bench to lead all rookies with 59 assists and 25 steals. She also averaged more than six points a game. She was named to the WNBA All-Rookie First Team.

Kristy Wallace

KELLY LOEFFLER
CO-OWNER
2011—21

GETTING POLITICAL

In December 2019, Georgia governor Brian Kemp appointed
Dream co-owner Kelly Loeffler to the U.S. Senate. She quickly
began a campaign to be elected by voters in the November 2020
general election. In July, she expressed her opposition to the
Black Lives Matter (BLM) movement. She claimed that it promoted
"violence and destruction across the country." The WNBA, whose
players are primarily black, had previously endorsed BLM. The
entire Dream roster, joined by many other players throughout
the league, openly expressed their opposition to Loeffler. They
campaigned for her opponent, the Reverend Raphael Warnock.
They wore T-shirts before games that said "Vote Warnock."
Warnock won. Players also successfully called for Loeffler's
removal from her ownership position.

ATLANTA DREAM

Rhyne Howard

The Dream were scheduled to have the third overall draft choice in the 2022 WNBA Draft. They traded up to secure the top pick. "We found a situation that made sense for us," said Dream general manager Dan Padover. "We've identified a player we feel very comfortable taking at No. 1. We went for it." That player turned out to be 6-foot-2 guard Rhyne Howard of the University of Kentucky (UK). She was the second-leading career scorer in UK history for both men and women. Atlanta especially liked her versatility. She could knock down three-pointers while posting up against most defenders. The Dream also drafted forward Naz Hillmon. She was the first player from the University of Michigan to be named an All-American.

Howard lived up to expectations. She was named to the All-Star Game. She finished the season with averages of 16.2 points, 4.5 rebounds, and 2.8 rebounds per game. She was named Rookie of the Month for all four months of the season. Howard sparked the team to a 4–1 start. Two months later Atlanta was 12–14 and still very much in playoff contention. The Dream won only two of the next nine games. They faced New York in the season's final game. The winner would claim the final playoff berth. Atlanta trailed just 80–79 with a minute left. But a New York three-point shot gave the Liberty a four-point edge. Atlanta closed to within two. Four Liberty free throws iced the game. Atlanta lost, 87–83.

The Atlanta Dream is one of the newest teams in the WNBA. In its 15 seasons, it has provided fans with some of the league's most exciting players. Even though Atlanta has fallen on hard times recently, fans are optimistic that the team will return to the highest levels in the standings.

Erica Wheeler

INDEX